# MAZE

*poem by*

# Matt Bialer

*Finishing Line Press*
Georgetown, Kentucky

# MAZE

Copyright © 2021 by Matt Bialer
ISBN 978-1-64662-533-8 First Edition
All rights reserved under International and Pan-American Copyright Conventions. No part of this book may be reproduced in any manner whatsoever without written permission from the publisher, except in the case of brief quotations embodied in critical articles and reviews.

## ACKNOWLEDGMENTS

I want to thank Mary Kathleen Flynn, Seb Doubinksky, Loretta Oleck and Finishing Line Press.

I also want to thank our wonderful daughter Izzy Bialer Lapidus.

Publisher: Leah Huete de Maines
Editor: Christen Kincaid
Cover Art: Matt Bialer
Author Photo: Mary Kathleen Flynn
Cover Design: Elizabeth Maines McCleavy

Order online: www.finishinglinepress.com
also available on amazon.com

Author inquiries and mail orders:
Finishing Line Press
PO Box 1626
Georgetown, Kentucky 40324
USA

*In memory of Lenora Lapidus: May 17, 1963—May 5, 2019*

I get an e-mail
From Michele
A & A Cemetery Services
And Memorials
Cemetery Lettering
Cleaning and Repairs
Rock Lettering
"Good morning
I wanted to
Let you know
The granite company
Must have been able
To get this completed
Before the shutdown
Rich was able
To get this monument
Set for you"
Set
The granite quarry
In Vermont
Ordered to shut down
COVID-19
Go into quarantine
Quarry in quarantine
"Get this monument
Set for you"
Set
Of course
I will go visit
Your monument
I designed myself
Want to see it
If it was

1

Done right
Done right
I will go later
To Ahavath Sholom Cemetery
Inside larger Elmwood Cemetery
Great Barrington, MA
When I am
On my grocery errands
Wear a scarf
Over my nose and mouth
Looking like a bandit
In this new normal
I can visit you
You're on the way
Looking like a bandit
Of course
I say tombstone
Rather than monument
Tombstone
Bandits and burial grounds
In Tombstone, Arizona
Tombstone, Arizona
Name means
Many things
To many people
Gunfights
Dusty streets
Whiskey
Faro card games
Wyatt Earp
Doc Holliday
Bandits and burial grounds
The granite quarry
In Vermont
Ordered to shut down
COVID-19
Go into quarantine
Quarry in quarantine
"Get this monument

Set for you"
Set
Tombstone, Arizona
Founded 1877
By Ed Schieffelin
Prospector
Staying at
What was then called
Camp Huachuca
(Wa-chu-ka)
Part of
Scouting expedition
Against Chiricahua Apaches
Would venture out
Into the desert
"Looking for rocks"
Ignoring warnings
From the soldiers
At the camp
About native Apaches
"Ed, the only stone
You will find out there
Will be your tombstone!"
Did discover his stones
Near Goose Flats
Silver
As a joke
Names his first mine
The Tombstone
Tombstone, Arizona
Bandits and burial grounds
The granite quarry
In Vermont
Ordered to shut down
COVID-19
Go into quarantine
Quarry in quarantine
"Get this monument
Set for you"

Set
Word spreads
About Ed's silver strike
Prospectors
Cowboys
Lawyers
Speculators
Gunmen
1879
A town site
Laid out
On a level spot
To the mines
Appropriately named
The new town
Tombstone
Tombstone, Arizona
Bandits and burial grounds
Within two years
Of its founding
Although very far
From any city
Has a bowling alley
4 churches
An ice house
2 banks
3 newspapers
Ice cream parlor
110 saloons
14 gambling halls
Numerous dance halls
And brothels
All situated among
And atop
Many silver mines
Gentlemen and ladies
Attend operas
Presented by visiting troupes
Schieffelin Hall

Opera House
Miners and cowboys
See shows
Bird Cage Theatre
And Brothel
Nowadays
The streets of Tombstone
Said to be
The pathways
Of many lingering spirits
Ghosts
Haunt the bullet-riddled Bird Cage
You can
Still see the smoke
A man moving along
In a long black frock coat
Often seen
Crossing the street
Where Virgil Earp
Was ambushed
Shot in the arm
Crippling him
For life
The man
In the long black frock coat
Never makes it
Across the street
Said to be the spirit of Earp
Never makes it
Across the street
You can
Still see the smoke
Bandits and burial grounds
The granite quarry
In Vermont
Ordered to shut down
COVID-19
Go into quarantine
Quarry in quarantine

"Get this monument
Set for you"
Set
A woman
In a long white dress
Spotted on
Tombstone streets
Fretful mother
Child died
From Yellow Fever
1880
Devastated
Later
Took her own life
Boot Hill Graveyard
Called such
Because so many
Of the occupants
Died with
Their boots on
Died with
With their boots on
Gunfights
Lawless past
Bandits and burial grounds
Men such as
Those killed in
OK Corral Gunfight
Marshal Fred White
Shot by Curly Bill Brocius
Charlie Storms
Murdered by Luke Short
Dozens more
Prospectors
Lawmen
Prostitutes
You can
Still see the smoke
Old cemetery

Fell into disrepair
Numerous
Old wooden tombstones
Falling down
Decomposing entirely
Visitors report
Blinking colored lights
Unidentifiable noises
Coming from the graveyard
People who die
And rise again
Rise like smoke
The man
In the long black frock coat
Never makes it
Across the street
Never makes it
Across the street
People who die
And rise again
Rise like smoke
Tombstone, Arizona
Bandits and burial grounds
The granite quarry
In Vermont
Ordered to shut down
COVID-19
Go into quarantine
Quarry in quarantine
"Get this monument
Set for you"
Set
I will go later
To Ahavath Sholom Cemetery
Inside larger Elmwood Cemetery
Great Barrington, MA
When I am
On my grocery errands
Wear a scarf

Over my nose and mouth
Looking like a bandit
In this new normal
I can visit you
You're on the way
Looking like a bandit
Of course
I say tombstone
Rather than monument
Tombstone

I watch
The Governor of New York
His daily news conference
Virus curve
On the descent
Looking to double
Daily virus testing
Truth
And facts
Truth
And facts
Make decisions
Based on facts
Some places
Have a different set
Of facts
A profound moment
We make a bad decision
It will set us back
We can't make
A bad decision
No time
To act stupid
Period
This will not
Be over
Any time soon
Will not

Be over
People want out
They want out
More people
Will die
If we are
Not smart
A marathon
Not a sprint
Test
Trace
Isolate
Coordinated tracing
35,000 medical students
Tristate
CUNY
SUNY
Test
Trace
Isolate
I take a shower
A psychologist
On the radio
The way
People will change
In response to it
Change in how
We think
And behave
And relate
To one another
What will
Our new normal
Feel like?
How do we
Find our way?
Do we ever
Get out of this?
A piece

Written by
One of my friend Mary's
Favorite priests
"When we are
No longer able
To change a situation
We are challenged
To change ourselves"
On the radio again
Funerals
Way we grieve
Will have to change
Change
My now virtual bereavement group
Zoom
Lisa
A public school teacher
Has lost friends
Friends of friends
"They can't
Have a real funeral
No cemetery event
They're just stuck
By themselves
At home
Alone with their grief
Alone
Imagine
If that happened
To us
Right after
Just imagine"
Funerals
Way we grieve
Will have to change
Change
"When we are
No longer able
To change a situation

We are challenged
To change ourselves"
Truth
And facts
Truth
And facts
We can't make
A bad decision
Test
Trace
Isolate
What will
Our new normal
Feel like?
How do we
Find our way?
Do we ever
Get out of this?

People who die
And rise again
Rise like smoke
The man
In the long black frock coat
Never makes it
Across the street
Never makes it
Across the street
People who die
And rise again
Rise like smoke
Tombstone, Arizona
Bandits and burial grounds
The granite quarry
In Vermont
Ordered to shut down
COVID-19
Go into quarantine
Quarry in quarantine

"Get this monument
Set for you"
Set
I will go later
To Ahavath Sholom Cemetery
Inside larger Elmwood Cemetery
Great Barrington, MA
When I am
On my grocery errands
Wear a scarf
Over my nose and mouth
Looking like a bandit
In this new normal
I can visit you
You're on the way
Looking like a bandit
Of course
I say tombstone
Rather than monument
Tombstone

An article
In the New York Times:
What Will Our New Normal
Feel Like?
Hints Are
Beginning to Emerge
"It was the first winter
That you realize
That this is going to last
This is your life"
A man named Velibor
Recalls of the 1990's
Siege of Sarajevo
Brought life
To a halt
Bosnian city
"And somehow you live
Just like people

Adapting to the situation now"
During 4 year siege
Sense of community
Memory
And time
All transformed
Transformed
Our ability
To focus
Feel more comfortable
Around others
To think
More than a few days
In advance
May diminish
Lasting consequences
Loss of control
One's normalcy
Freedom
Face-to-face connection
Sarajevo siege survivors
Heightened sense
Of special awareness
Ability to
Evade bullets
Bombs
People will change
In response to it
Change in how
We think
And behave
And relate
To one another
What will
Our new normal
Feel like?
 "When we are
No longer able
To change a situation

We are challenged
To change ourselves"
Funerals
Way we grieve
Will have to change
Change
Velibor
Sarajevo survivor
A street
Near his home
Often targeted
By snipers
Avoided during war
And well after
Well after
Didn't walk that street
For a long time
Blinking colored lights
Unidentifiable noises
Coming from the graveyard
People who die
And rise again
Rise like smoke
The man
In the long black frock coat
Never makes it
Across the street
Never makes it
Across the street
People who die
And rise again
Rise like smoke
Siege of Sarajevo
Sniper Alley
Named primarily
For streets
Zmaja od Bosne Street
Dragon of Bosnia Street
And Mesa Selimovic Boulevard

Main drag
Of the city
Lined with snipers
Connects industrial sections
To the Old Town's cultural
And historic sites
High-rise buildings
Giving snipers
Extensive fields
Of fire
Extensive fields
Of fire
Mountains surrounding
The city
Also used
For sniper positions
Providing a safe distance
Excellent views
Maze of streets
And targets
Although
City under constant attack
People still able
To move about
In order
To survive
Routinely
Risking their lives
Signs reading
"Pazi – Snaijper!"
Watch out – Sniper!
People either
Run fast
Across the street
Or wait
For United Nations
Armored vehicles
Using them
As shields

Visitors report
Blinking colored lights
Unidentifiable noises
Coming from the graveyard
People who die
And rise again
Rise like smoke
The man
In the long black frock coat
Never makes it
Across the street
Never makes it
Across the street
People who die
And rise again
Rise like smoke
The way
People will change
In response to it
Change in how
We think
And behave
And relate
To one another
What will
Our new normal
Feel like?
How do we
Find our way?
Do we ever
Get out of this?
Only one
Functioning hotel
During the siege
Holiday Inn
49,000 beds
For the 1984 Winter Olympics
Foreign journalists
Stayed in the hotel

Great number
Of rooms
Burnt or destroyed
Walls blown apart
The most prized rooms
Those without a view
Of the mountains
A view of the mountains
A view of a sniper's nest
If you see him
He sees you
We went
To Sarajevo
1990
Two years
Before the siege
We had no idea
Everything so quaint
And normal
Mix of east and west
Spectacular natural beauty
Of the city
Best way to see it
Find the highest
Vantage point possible
Take a cable car
From the Olympics
Up the mountainside
Foothills of
Mount Trebevic
Lifted us
1100 meters
In seven minutes
Breathtaking views
From the top
Shifting kaleidoscope
Cityscape sweltering
Clear blue sky
Quickly became obscured

Twirling strands
Of mist
And fog
Appear from nowhere
Mosques
Minarets
Romanesque towers
Of Catholic churches
Onion shaped domes
Of Orthodox churches
Little did we know
We would be
Up where the snipers
Would soon roam
From this idyllic
Picture postcard backdrop
Down in the city
We wandered
Cobblestone streets
Bascarsija
Old Bezistan
Open fronted cafes
Strong Bosnian coffee
Hookah pipes
Café Ramis
Windows open fully
On the street
Relaxing inside
With our guide books
Coffee
Ottoman geometric pattern
Viennese Sachertorte
Krempita Kolac
Custard slice
At the vast bazaar
Among the booths
Of the metal craftsmen
We bought
A coffee set

Coated with brass
Engraved metal
Gold and silver trim
Spoons
Coffee carafe
Sugar bowl
From this idyllic
Picture postcard backdrop
Nowadays
On the bazaar
One can buy
Intricately engraved
Shell casings
From the siege
Perhaps
Most poignant keepsake
A simple postcard
Many of them
Being sold today
Panoramic photos
Of the city
Taken from
The numerous new graveyards
From the war
In the surrounding hills
Breathtaking views
From the top
Shifting kaleidoscope
Cityscape sweltering
Clear blue sky
Quickly became obscured
Twirling strands
Of mist
And fog
Appear from nowhere
Excellent views
Maze of streets
And targets
Although

City under constant attack
People still able
To move about
In order
To survive
Routinely
Risking their lives
Signs reading
"Pazi – Snaijper!"
Watch out – Sniper!
Great number
Of rooms
Burnt or destroyed
Walls blown apart
The most prized rooms
Those without a view
Of the mountains
A view of the mountains
A view of a sniper's nest
If you see him
He sees you
People will change
In response to it
Change in how
We think
And behave
And relate
To one another
What will
Our new normal
Feel like?
How do we
Find our way?
Do we ever
Get out of this?
 "When we are
No longer able
To change a situation
We are challenged

To change ourselves"
Funerals
Way we grieve
Will have to change
Change
Truth
And facts
Truth
And facts
We can't make
A bad decision
Test
Trace
Isolate
What will
Our new normal
Feel like?
People who die
And rise again
Rise like smoke
The man
In the long black frock coat
Never makes it
Across the street
Never makes it

People who die
And rise again
Rise like smoke
Tombstone, Arizona
Bandits and burial grounds
Not long
Before you died
We watched
The first season
Of Westworld
On HBO
The mysterious
Man in Black

Searches for
The center
Of the Maze
Seen throughout the park
Branding irons
Plowed
Into a field
Drawn into the ground
On coffins
A tabletop
Inside the scalp
Of Kissy
A faro and blackjack dealer
Mariposa Salon
Throat savagely cut
By the Man in Black
A design of the Maze
Embedded in his scalp
Revelation of Akecheta tattooing
The Maze design
Inside the scalp
Indicates Kissy
A member of the Ghost Nation
People here die
Are repaired
Returned to life
The Maze
There's something
Dolores should try
It's a game
It's called the Maze
Representation
For creating consciousness
For being sentient
People here die
Are repaired
Returned to life
Man in Black
Searches for clues

About the Maze
Dives deeper
Into Westworld
The Maze
The goal
Of the game
Is to find
The center
Of the Maze
At which point
Dolores
Will become sentient
Sentient
And free
In some circles
The Maze is
Rumored to be
Sum of man's life
At its center
Lies a man
Who has been killed
Over and over
Only to come back
To life
To keep out
His oppressors
He built The Maze
People who die
And rise again
Rise like smoke
The man
In the long black frock coat
Never makes it
Across the street
Never makes it
Across the street
People who die
And rise again
Rise like smoke

I go on
My grocery errands
Then go to the cemetery
To see your monument
To Ahavath Sholom
Inside larger Elmwood Cemetery
Great Barrington, MA
Your tombstone
Windy
Clouding up fast
Trees starting to bud
Hills come alive
Tombstones spread out
Across the grass
Like they can breathe
Your tombstone
The top
From a poem you wrote:
THESE TREES, THESE HILLS:
TAKE A GOOD LOOK
Your name
Date of birth
Date of death
CIVIL RIGHTS CHAMPION
I stare
At your tombstone
Take some photos
With my phone
Gray granite
Big gray wall
Between life
And death
Now I know
What they mean
By "set in stone"
The granite quarry
In Vermont
Ordered to shut down
COVID-19

Go into quarantine
Quarry in quarantine
"Get this monument
Set for you"
Set
Your death so real
So set
Big gray wall
Between life
And death
Between us
I feel sad
Your death so real
So set
I wish
You can be repaired
Returned to life
At its center
Lies a man
Who has been killed
Over and over
Only to come back
To life

The drive back
It's getting cloudy
Fog settling in
Over the hills
And pastures
I drive past
Summer Street
By High Lawn Farm
A memory
Late summer
2018
You had been ill
Your oncologist
Was worried
You might not make it

Might not make it
Through the summer
Dangerously low platelets
Concerned about a heart attack
Brain bleeds
Very tricky chemo treatment
Targeted at your bone marrow
Lots of rules
Disinfecting wipes
No teeth flossing
No chopping vegetables
"Let your husband do it"
No kayak rides
But you rallied once again
Made it through
And we were
So happy
So happy
As a kind of reward
For both of us
You wanted to
Take me
To a special spot
Off Summer Street
You passed
As you were driving
For gyrotonics in Lee
"You have to see it
And take lots of pictures
So you can paint it"
You directed me
In the car
We got out
Storm clouds
Over the hills
Wind
"Better get
Those pictures in!
Hurry!"

Blue gray clouds
Over dark green hills
Fog
"Do you like it?
Do you like it?
Was I right?"
You chuckle
Yes you were
I like this
I'm going to paint it
For you
For you
"I told ya!"
I drive past
Summer Street
Which I can't
Drive down
Maybe ever again
Memories
Are like snipers
Signs reading
"Pazi – Snaijper!"
Watch out – Sniper!
Great number
Of rooms
Burnt or destroyed
Walls blown apart
The most prized rooms
Those without a view
Of the mountains
A view of the mountains
A view of a sniper's nest
If you see him
He sees you
I can't go there
Too sad
Too sad
As I drive back
More fog

Descends
I think
Of your tombstone
The cemetery
THESE TREES, THESE HILLS:
TAKE A GOOD LOOK
Covered in fog
Uncertain
Insubstantial
Disembodied
Soft and fluid
Gray walls
Gray building
Empty streets
"Pazi – Snaijper!"
The tombstones
March down
From the hills
People who die
And rise again
Rise like smoke
All of this COVID
And grief
Like trying to
Escape from a maze
When I get home
I ask Izzy
If she wants
To see the photos
Of your tombstone
"No, I can't look
I can't"
Fog on the mind
I go down
To the basement
Paint a watercolor landscape
Bare winter trees
Against a hill
Shrouded in fog

Bare trees
Fog on the mind
The cemetery
THESE TREES, THESE HILLS:
TAKE A GOOD LOOK
Covered in fog
Uncertain
Insubstantial
Disembodied
Soft and fluid
Gray walls
Gray building
Empty streets
"Pazi – Snaijper!"
The tombstones
March down
From the hills
People who die
And rise again
Rise like smoke
You and me
On Summer Street
Late summer 2018
Smiling
Laughing
Happy to be alive
And together
Storm clouds
And fog
Over the lush distant hills
There is no cemetery

Matt Bialer is the author of more than a dozen books of poetry including ALWAYS SAY GOODNIGHT (KYSO Flash), ASCENT and WONDER WEAVERS (JournalStone) and THE VALLEY OF THE EIGHT and THIRD EYE OF THE INNER LIGHT (Leaky Boot Press). His poems have appeared in many print and online journals, including *Cultural Weekly, Forklift Ohio, Green Mountains Review, H_NGM_N, Le Zaporogue* and *MacQueen's Quinterly*.

In addition, Matt is an acclaimed street photographer (primarily black and white) who has exhibited his work widely. Some of his images are held in the permanent collections of The Brooklyn Museum, The Museum of the City of New York and The New York Public Library. He is also an accomplished watercolor landscape painter with works in many private collections and "best of" books. He lives in Park Slope, Brooklyn.

www.ingramcontent.com/pod-product-compliance
Lightning Source LLC
LaVergne TN
LVHW041512070426
835507LV00012B/1523